T0163790

MILESTONES

POEMS OF
LIFE AND LOVE

KATHRYN CAROLE ELLISON

Published by Lady Bug Books, an imprint of Brisance Books Group.
Lady Bug Press and the distinctive ladybug logo are registered trademarks of
Lady Bug Books, LLC.

Lady Bug Books
400 112th Avenue N.E.
Suite 230
Bellevue, WA 98004
www.giftsoflove.com

For information about custom editions, special sales and permissions, please contact
Brisance Books Group at specialsales@brisancebooksgroup.com

Manufactured in the United States of America
ISBN: 978-1-944194-58-1

First Edition: May 2019

A NOTE FROM THE AUTHOR

The poems in this book were written over many years as gifts to my children. I began writing them in the 1970s, when they were reaching the age of reason. And, as I found myself in the position of becoming a single parent, I wanted to do something special to share with them—something that would become a tradition, a ritual they could count on.

And so the Advent Poems began—one day, decades ago—with a poem 'gifted' to them each day during the Advent period leading up to Christmas, December 1 to December 24. Forty some years later... my children still look forward each year to the poems that started a family tradition, that new generations have come to cherish.

It is my sincere hope that you will embrace and enjoy them, and share them with those you love.

Children of the Light was among the early poems I wrote, and is included in each of the *Poems of Life and Love* books in The Ellison Collection: *Heartstrings, Celebrations, Inspirations, Sanctuary, Awakenings, Sojourns, Milestones, Tapestry* and *Gratitude*. After writing many hundreds of poems, it is still my favorite. The words came from my heart... and my soul... and flowed so effortlessly that it was written in a single sitting. All I needed to do was capture the words on paper.

Light, to me, represented all that was good and pure and right with the world, and I believed then—as I do today—that those elements live in my children, and perhaps in all of us. We need only to dare.

– KCE

Dedication

To my parents: Herb and Bernice Haas

Mom, you were the poet who went before me...
unpublished, but appreciated nonetheless.

And Dad, you always believed in me,
no matter what direction my life took.
Thank you for your faith in me,
and for your unconditional love.

TABLE OF CONTENTS

LIFE'S JOYS

LIFE'S LESSONS

LIFE'S GIFTS

LIFE'S JOYS

AT EIGHTY

As an intro to MILESTONES, I thought it would be
Of interest to share memories from my diary.
And though I'm "unique," my life's much the same
As others who live through events and are still "in the game."

There are wisdoms and thoughts I'd like to pass along,
And I sing them loudly, for they are my life's song:
You can't help getting older, but you don't have to get old.
Keep your mind young, and don't always do what you're told.

Becoming eighty is merely a matter of life and death.
I choose life, and I'll live it to my very last breath.
In my dreams I'm never eighty years old.
My adventures as I sleep are marvelous to behold.

Now, granted, at eighty, my birthday suit needs pressing,
But as I look around I am happily processing
The knowledge I've accumulated throughout my years,
And the joys of sharing them now, without fears.

The biggest advantage of living to this age
Is the time to acquire people to love at each stage.
In my youth there were people of action and adventure;
The more physical the activity, the more excitement, to be sure.

And later I found friends who were seeking something more...
A reason for existence beyond 'minding the store.'
What is my purpose? What does it all mean?
The questions were large. The answers unseen.

Time has a way of moving things along.
Some answers came slowly and some poured headlong.
Enough to learn I must share what I know,
Starting with family, then others to follow.

It takes a long lifetime to grow young once more;
From birth through youth, to a full four score.
The advantage of living to 80 and more?
There are more people to love, but who's keeping score?

At 80,
Jessica Tandy won a Best Actress Oscar,
Yuichiro Miura climbed Mt. Everest,
and Coco was still running Chanel.
There's life still to be lived!

CHILDREN OF THE LIGHT

There are those souls who bring the light,
Who spill it out for all to share.
And with a joy that does excite,
They show the world that they do care.
It is so very bright.

In this sharing, love does pervade
Into their lives and cycles round;
And as this light is outward played
The love is also inward bound.
It is an awesome trade.

You are a soul whose light is shared.
It comes from deep within your heart.
It's best because it is not spared,
Because it's total, not just part.
And I am glad you've dared.

CONTROL WHAT YOU CAN

There are things you can control,
And there are things to just ignore.
You're not meant to have a hand on
Every detail... what a chore!

You are a person who is caring,
And you feel another's woes.
You want to help them if you can;
To help them fight their unseen foes.

But take a breath before you leap;
The urge to help may need reviewing.
Don't lay claims to things for which
You've no control or business doing.

To allow another to work through
His/Her situation may just be
The best way you can be of help.
Let go the reins... and wait and see.

FRIENDS AND FAMILY

(A Love Letter to My Children)

Sometimes I think that I am just
About the luckiest woman I know.
You two and I are friends and family.
I really love you so.

You open up and share with me
Your feelings and your dreams.
And I, in turn, share mine with you—
It's more rare than it seems.

Stay opened up and unafraid
And keep the channels wide.
More good things will come to you
If you keep nothing locked inside.

It's a risk, my loves, to let people know you.
They're used to digging and prying,
Then walking away dissatisfied,
And making up a story—lying
About who someone else really is,
Forgetting that person's an extension
Of themselves and everything else that is.
The problems reach an unreal dimension.

One thing I've found to be true in my life
Is that when I'm unafraid and let go,
And let people know who I really am,
They, in turn, open up and let me know
Who they are, what they want, and what they believe.
It's generally not much different than me.
When they can trust, they love the chance
To let it all out and be free.

We're each unique in the ways we show
The love that is deep inside;
But, it's oh, so nice to let it out
And never have to hide.

PASSION

Great artists or dancers are not great from technique;
They are great because of the passion for their art.
Passion is energy. It keeps you on track.
It's the reason for your success. It sets you apart.

Passion gets you through the hardest of times,
When you might be convinced to just give up.
Passion gives meaning and depth to your life.
Go for the gusto, and don't ever let up.

There is no passion to be found in playing small;
In settling for a life that is less than your dreams.
Whatever you do, do it with determination.
Stay focused and passionate... for your own self-esteem.

Since passion is energy, feel the power that comes
From focusing on what excites you the most.
A passion for learning will guarantee continued growth.
Living from passion is fulfilling as you come to each milepost.

LEARNING

Those who stop learning new things become "old."
The world, ever changing, passes them by.
To rehash information that has been updated
Is an exercise for memory only, whereby
A true learning begins by opening your mind
And always asking the question, "Why?"

Learning begins at the moment you're born
And should continue to your very last breath.
The secret to living a youthful life
Is to learn, continuously, until your death.
Be open to new things, learn about them well
Before they're deleted from your experiential "net."

In the process of learning about things of the world
You are put into a most ideal position
To find out new things about yourself
And about others in the world—the human condition.
Curiosity is the key: always ask questions,
And the collection of knowledge will be your tradition.

AGING

A lot has been said about the aging process
By people down through the centuries.
Aging is something that happens to us all
In spite of the Botox®, the facelifts, or new knees.

As children we worried that youth would last forever.
Our dreams were about being older and more wise.
We plotted and planned about what it would be like
When we finally could fit into clothes, parents' size.

Wearing Mama's big dress and high-heeled shoes
Or Daddy's hat that came down to our nose,
We play-acted adult roles; we made up scenarios
Of what kinds of rules on our children we'd impose.

Looking forward with hope to futures so bright,
Dreaming fantasies without any limit,
We made our way through the early years,
Lost in our dreams that were indefinite.

First to get through grade school, and then on to "high,"
(I don't mean the artificially induced kind here)
Then to college and marriage and "happily ever after."
Our dreams were vast–to the stratosphere!

It all came true, in one form or another!
Aging brought experiences and molded our lives.
We graduated, we worked to put food on the table,
And many of us acquired either husbands or wives.

But did some dreams die with each stage that we passed:
Did they disappear right into thin air?
The dreams that we had before we grew up–
Did we lose them for good? If not, where?

I believe, somehow, we still have them inside.
I believe we've not lost them (a statement bold).
But, if so, remember these words and ponder:
"When your memories outweigh your dreams, you're old!"

(YOUR) AUTOBIOGRAPHY

It's said that every artist writes
His own story through what he produces.
Autobiography is always about the stories
Told through what the artist introduces.

Autobiography has taken a bad rap.
Some call it indulgent while others call it lying.
It's the story of how a person thinks he lived,
And the things with which he was identifying.

Auden wrote that there are two characters
In every autobiography that's penned.
There's Don Quixote, the Ego, the showman;
And Sancho Panza, the Self, he would contend.

It's also been said that autobiography reveals nothing bad
About its writer except, perhaps, his memory.
What if everyone was required to write about his life?
If everyone took stock, would it change history?

E. M. FORSTER SPEAKS FOR ME

Causes come and causes go—
It all depends on who's in power.
It's rally around for some politician
Or give to save the Leaning Tower.
It's defend the left or lean to the right;
Neither one deserves my attention.
What's important to me is being and sharing
With people of good intention.
There are causes and there is friendship,
And if they agree it's fine—
But if the causes lose their kindliness,
Then, thank you, I decline.
If I should ever have to choose
Between my government and my friend,
I intend to have the guts to say,
"Ta ta, Government. On you I can't depend.".

LOOK TO YOUR HEARTS

LOOK TO YOUR HEARTS—to your very core
And trust its reading on every score.
If you learn to read your true messages there
You'll do good things, and avoid despair.

LEARN FROM THE ARTS—they're our past and our future.
They keep our culture alive, they might be the cure
Of all the world's ills, if given a chance—
Painting and poetry and music and dance.

DON'T MEASURE YOUR FEATS—just note them, that's all.
Before you can run, you must learn to crawl.
Each new thing you learn adds to what you know.
Just take it in stride as your accomplishments grow.

DON'T COUNT YOUR RECEIPTS, at least toward self-worth.
You're worth much more; you were, even at birth.
You gain self-worth not by what you get each day.
Oh no, you gain it by what you give away.

MEASURE LOVE IN HEARTBEATS, not in trinkets or dollars.
The true magnitude of love can evade even scholars.
Let the magic of love take away your fears,
And to your life of happiness you'll add many years.

IGNORE TALLY SHEETS. At the end of the day
Love is not measured on paper—no way!
It's in your hearts; it will always be there.
It feeds your soul even more when you share.

YES, TRUE LOVE STARTS deep inside in your being.
You may look outside, but it's not love you are seeing,
But a reflection of what you hold inside.
Take a personal inventory, your heart to guide.

WHEN JUDGMENT DEPARTS it opens the door
To share your love, to watch it soar.
You'll live happier when you're not looking outside
For the truest love. Let your heart be your guide.

GET IN THE GAME

The game of life has its ups and downs.
You come to expect its variations.
When it goes down, when the going gets harder
It's time to "up your game," without hesitations.

Do not lose focus of your individual goal.
Keep your efforts strong... to the heights you aim.
You cannot change the cards you are dealt.
You can control only how you play the game.

Every day has its new opportunity;
You can build on yesterday's success. Yes, you can.
Or start over fresh from a different direction,
With a new way to play. Be an Olympian!

Risk is always a part of your program.
If you don't take chances, the outcome's the same.
You can't hit a home run sitting there wishing.
Get off the bench—and Get In The Game!

A LITTLE DARK HUMOR

The following is attributed to
None other than Oscar Wilde.
(He lived a very colorful life
That was anything but mild.)

"The Gods have two ways of dealing with us..."
"Harshly," completes his theorem.
"The first way is to deny us our dreams;
And the second is to grant them."

The way that his words ring true for me
—The words from this fabulous wit—
Is that sometimes we think we'll not succeed;
And then when we do, we quit!

EXPLORATIONS

Mankind has legs—no plant nor tree
To bind us to one place forever!
Mankind can wander, and wander he must.
Staying in one place? The ties must sever!

We were given legs with which to wander
And explore the world around that we share
With all of nature, including (other) human beings,
And places and thoughts and dreams everywhere!

Our views of science should be never-ending.
There, so far, has been no ultimate end to the mystery.
There are mysteries in nature, there are new worlds to conquer.
It's the journey that matters throughout history.

Do not grow old, no matter your age.
Move like curious children to explore your surroundings,
Because somewhere something incredible awaits your gaze.
You get a new way of seeing that is astounding!

It's good to have an end to journey toward,
But it's the journey that matters, in the end.
Keep on exploring, keep on evolving.
Life is one grand adventure, my friends.

... AND THE GREATEST OF THESE IS CHARITY

"Faith, Hope, and Love: these three...
And the greatest of these is Charity."
Words that are written on many pages;
Wisdom that lasts throughout the ages;
The magnitude of which you will agree.

To live one's life with an eye to find
Others who have been left behind;
And then to assist them along their way
So they can thrive another day...
Is a blessing for all mankind.

LIFE'S LESSONS

HUXLEY, SIMPLIFIED

Goals are set with hopes of attainment,
And to those ends we strive.
The way we strive is important here,
To the quality of how we survive.

The end can never justify the means,
For the simple and obvious explanation:
That the means employed determine the nature
Of the ends produced—a manifestation.

Silence

Comfortable silence is very rare.
It is best when love enhanced.
It is a measure for gauging how far
A relationship has advanced.

In conversation, an occasional silence
Can be compared to a meat marinating.
It allows the flavor to soak in and season
With the love and the feelings cascading.

Sometimes, when challenged, there is temptation
To respond, talking like some nut.
But usually the better part of wisdom
Is to keep your mouth firmly shut!

Well chosen words have been known to change
The course of history, north and south.
But sometimes the worst thing you can do
For another is to open your mouth.

MATURITY

The distilled experience of men of all ages
Has resulted in discoveries about mature living.
And, having said this, and digested the lore,
The information now is mine for the giving.

Your basic direction is toward wholeness of life—
Like a tree, you should grow from the center.
A great life is built on enduring values.
Of your bodies, your soul is the renter.

No outstanding work is accomplished alone.
It takes all of us working shoulder to shoulder.
Miracles occur when it is not important
Just who puts the credit in his folder.

You should not dodge reality or turn your back
On life's unpleasant beat.
Private bravery is the price you must pay
For your personal victory so sweet.

To be too elated or discouraged about life,
Robert Louis Stevenson says is bad form.
He instructs "to go on in fortune and misfortune
Like a clock in a thunderstorm."

Time is the great healer of hurts and sorrows.
New doors open if you don't lose heart.
Learn to distinguish between important and not;
(That's not always the easiest part).

It is wiser to judge a man by his life
Than by what he says aloud.
It is better to follow one's own higher aims
Than to go along with the crowd.

Moderation in all things is a good rule to follow;
It's wise to walk in balance on your road.
No one can enslave you; you are free to live
By a forever reaching higher, personal code.

YOUR AUTHENTIC LIFE

If your beliefs about yourself
Are valid and undoubted,
You'll live with self-perception strong...
Your praises may be shouted.
You'll be dynamic in all you do;
And with all of your communications.
Your credibility will speak for itself.
You'll have no limitations.

You've met such people in your travels...
Larger than life, their bearing.
They experience life with so much color:
With excitement, élan and daring...
With enthusiasm they make life fun
And laughter fills the air.
Through them we see authentic life.
And it's yours, if you but dare.

Sort your life between fact and fiction;
To seek your authentic being.
Be ruthless about discarding what's false...
The exercise is freeing.
Then live consistently with who you are.
Don't settle for anything less.
Be genuine in everything you do.
You'll experience great success.

RELATIONSHIPS

In my childhood I wanted to believe in the idea
Of soul mates, and of love at first sight.
I was warned to be careful with my heart,
But still wished for a soul mate with all of my might.

Taking on the attitude of never giving up,
I searched high and low for Mr. Right.
I wanted him to be perfect, to provide for all my needs.
In my dreams, he was that... but in daylight?

When I no longer believed in the idea of soul mates,
Or love at first sight, or perfection,
It opened the possibilities of finding a mate
Who could pass my relaxed inspection.

After a while I realized that my dream mate might
Have flaws, be wrong, and still be perfect
For the imperfect me, with all my flaws.
His `wrongness` with mine, would connect.

We are all incomplete, we're always searching
For somebody to complete us, to make us whole.
Still unfulfilled, after a period of time
We blame, and find others to seek our goal.

Serial polygamy can go on for years
Until we admit we are solely responsible
For our own fulfillment. our love of self.
Till then, each relationship is collapsible.

Even then, there cannot be a healthy relationship
Unless there is loyalty and commitment.
Relationships require love, patience and persistence.
Trust is the foundation, the base element.

RIGHT THINKING

The mind is not a vessel to be filled.
Oh no, it's a fire to be kindled.
We thought that teaching would make us smart...
In fact, man's ability to think has dwindled.

The essence of the independent mind lies not
In what it thinks... but how...
To strengthen your intellect, don't get lost in opinion.
Let your mind be a thoroughfare. It knows how.

"We cannot solve your problems with the same level of thinking
That created them..." So says Einstein.
A public opinion poll is no substitute for thought!
(We forget that some of the time.)

The world you have created is a process of your thinking.
It cannot be changed until you change your thought.
You are responsible for both what you do and think,
Because action follows thinking... it's what you have brought.

At the time between thought and action you can elect
To stop whatever path might be a wrong choice.
Don't fall into the trap of believing all your thoughts.
Hold out for the ones which have a pure voice.

William James said it well when he made the statement
About the greatest weapon against stress.
He said it's your ability to choose one thought
Over another ... (a pathway to wellness).

GOING AROUND, COMING AROUND

Whatever you send out to the universe—
Your words, your moods, your belief—
Will either come back as pleasure
Or will be destined to give you grief.

If you desire more love and compassion
And peace of mind in your life,
Then create that reality for yourself,
And end all that inner strife.

Be more loving, compassionate, and peaceful.
Your joy and happiness will abound.
You create your own reality, right?
What goes around, comes around.

PLAYING YOUR ROLE

What role in life have you selected for yourself?
And in what style are you going to play it?
Divine Will has a hand in assigning our role,
But choices we make can weight it.

Some of us will act in only a short drama,
And for some, the performance will be long—
The roles we accept must be played to perfection.
If it's difficult, remember, complaining is wrong!

Wherever you find yourself in your life's role,
Give an impeccable performance. Do your best!
Whatever your role, play it with all your might.
Enjoy your life! In yourself, invest!

TRAVELERS

On a flight recently there was an old man
Who was rude and loud and scary.
I couldn't help but notice him.
He was really quite contrary.

He demanded this and demanded that.
He spoke so bluntly and rough.
He wouldn't smile, his voice was mean.
His manner was very tough.

The attendant gave him what he demanded
(She was so very nice.)
I, on the other hand, might have "had enough,"
And laced his food with spice.

She practiced the art of patient love.
She thought well of him in her heart.
She was an angel from whom I learned
That living well, and right, is an art.

He calmed right down when he realized
That she was there for him, within reason.
He even smiled... I heard him laugh.
His troubles, they were easing.

Life's lessons appear when least expected,
Even on a routine trip.
Be alert to every opportunity to observe,
And relish the joy of companionship.

COMMITMENTS

The secret to being happy in this life
Is to follow with action what you say,
But don't expect others to act in kind—
It just may not be their way.

You can't control other people's actions,
But are in complete control of your own.
You must keep your word, your promises,
Or over time you'll set a negative tone.

It starts with self-doubt, an uncomfortable feeling
Which feeds your sense of "no value."
It causes tiredness, with confusion galore,
And robs you of knowing the "real" you.

The result of this unpleasantness usually follows
With your sense of self-worth down the drain.
The feeling of "I can't do anything,"
Surrounds every task. There's no gain.

To reverse this negative flow of your life,
A few simple steps must be taken.
First, don't make commitments you cannot keep.
Your credibility would be shaken.

Make only those that are important to you.
They're the ones you're more likely to keep,
And then follow through, make sure they are done.
You're more apt to get a good night's sleep.

ARGUMENTS

If you use your words as a sword
You can always expect a duel;
And the louder the volume of words in use
The more likely you'll play the fool.

Because arguing does to the spirit, my dears,
What disease can do to the body—
And an unhealthy spirit can give you... what?
A life that's bound to be shoddy.

The greater number of words you use,
The less likely they are to be heard.
The greatest amount of impact comes
From carefully choosing each word.

Words are where most fights begin
Over when, wherefore, or whether—
My advice is this: the brain and the mouth
Are meant to work together.

THE POWER TO CHANGE

The single greatest power you have
Today is the power to change some things.
If what you see is out of whack
Then you must pull some ˙altering˙ strings.

It would be grossly irresponsible for you
To let it continue as status quo.
Change is required in order that
You will have a better tomorrow.

All existence is in a perpetual flux
Of being and growing into something new.
That's what is known as evolution;
There are times that change depends on you.

LIFE

Life cannot be "reduced to size."
Unlike sticks or stones or stars or space,
It goes beyond things that simply "are."
Life's the ultimate miracle for you to embrace.

Have you wept at anything within the past year?
Has the sight of young beauty made your heart race?
Do you see with your heart as well as with your eyes;
Do you carry a smile upon your face?

Have you thought seriously about the fact
That some day you'll finally lay down and die?
That the time you have on earth right now
Is yours to waste or to occupy?

More often than not, do you really listen
When people are speaking to you from their heart?
Or do you only half hear their stories
As you wait impatiently, your own tale to impart?

Is there anyone you know in whose place you would step
If he were faced with suffering great loss or pain?
If you couldn't change places with him, would you listen
As he holds your hand, your comfort to obtain?

Ask yourself these questions; it's crucial for you
To search your heart, and also your head.
If your answer to most of these questions is "No,"
Then the chances are that you're already dead.

ENGAGE YOUR CURIOSITY

In order to have a love affair with life
And a reason to get out of bed each morning...
And, further, a purpose to keep moving with joy,
Live as variously as possible... take warning!

Learn as much as you can about all that is good,
And follow your nose for even more than you see.
Climb aboard the Curiosity Train
And roar across the land with "joie de vivre."

All life began as a mystery and will
End as mystery no matter what you do...
But what about your time in between?
Fill your life and soul... it's up to you!

Design a "workout," and then follow it well
To keep your curiosity healthy and fit.
What exercises would you include in your plan?
It's easy, you know. Make a list and do it!

LIFE'S GIFTS

Q & A

Q

To what do you owe your great success
In living life so long?
How do you manage the spring in your step?
How do you stay so strong?

Why do you wake up ready to go
In so many exciting directions?
Aren't you always having to make
A large number of corrections?

What is the reason you always have the time
To pursue so many interests?
Is there no limit to your appetite
For passing new personal tests?

A

The fundamental precept of
The path to a life that's long
Is to avoid satiety.
Complacency is wrong.

One must not lose desires in life.
They stimulate what is new.
Creativity is stimulated when
One sees through eyes that are new.

Possessing desires is a sure way
To stay in love all your life.
To live long and to love are worthwhile aims.
May you reach them without undue strife.

A LIFE WITHOUT PASSION?

A life without passion is no life at all.
You've heard these words before.
But, reading or hearing is only one step
Toward grasping meaning, and furthermore,
Here are more words to support this proposal,
The truth of which I have no doubt:
If you have no purpose, you have no passion.
And without passion, you've sold yourself out.

If cynicism and apathy are regular moods
That endanger your daily routine,
It's because you've abandoned yourself and what matters...
Lost the truth of what might have been.

Passion, excitement and confidence are
Essential elements for everyday living.
They're necessary to your peace of mind,
And a joyous exchange you are giving.

When you are passionate the others around you
Feed off your amazing dance.
They absorb your bounce and give it right back,
And joy is not left to chance.

HONOR YOUR ANCESTORS

From your ancestors you inherit many things.
You take them for granted, in all probabilities;
The color of your eyes, the texture of your hair–
And the unfolding of varied interests and abilities.

Think about the name you are given at birth.
It might have come from your great grand–something.
Your last name, for sure, carries your father's mark.
From the past to the present, there is a string.

Within your fragile vessels of skin and bone cells
You carry with you this inheritance of being.
You are links between the ages, and contain expectations
Of the past to the future line of guaranteeing.

You hold both sacred memories
And future promise, though at times unclear.
Only when you recognize that you are an heir
Can you be free to be a pioneer.

LOOK INSIDE

If all the world has gone awry—
If life is one big alibi—
If things come up that make you cry—
… Just look inside for the answer.

If things go wrong on a daily basis—
If all you see are angry faces—
If people are always on your cases—
… Just look inside for the answer.

It is through our own self-discovery
That the world will make its recovery—
And "luck" won't seem such a lottery.
… Just look inside for the answer.

THE HAPPINESS HABIT

Happiness is such a nebulous thing—
It comes and goes on a whim.
It's pretty much where you find it;
It depends on where you 'swim.'

Since there's nothing more invigorating
Than to share a happy space,
Be sure to put yourself with people
Who wear a happy face.

A contribution you can make
Which will add to the happiness habit
Is to make sure your words fall gently
Upon another's spirit.

Gracious words add beauty
To the environment, yes they do.
Like begets like, so say kind words.
Happiness begins with you.

And what is true, this one last thing,
Which I will now append:
Your happiness is bound to be doubled
When you share it with a friend.

CHANGE

Change implies the passing from the old to the new,
But it must produce a change of mind, too.
Going from place to place doesn't produce a shift
Unless your mind changes—you get my drift.

A renewal of mind produces greater good,
With better health and more happiness, in all likelihood.
A constant renewal—the daily change of mind
Is possible to everyone—to all of mankind.

In all the world, change is the greatest remedy.
Unwillingness to change could end in tragedy;
And we are always the change that we seek.
Change is the law of life—so perfect your technique.

Change is the end result of all true learning...
You know it can be better—you are constantly yearning.
And the way to make sense out of change is to take a chance.
Plunge into it, move with it. Enjoy the dance.

If you don't change direction you'll end up where you're heading;
Not going anywhere exactly, mostly treading.
You can change the world with the power of your vision.
Don't underestimate its power—make the decision.

THE GIFT OF PROSPERITY

Prosperity is one of those concepts which requires
Its opposite in order to fully understand
The meaning, with all of its nuances and elements,
So bear with me as I further expand.

The opposite, of course, is adversity—you know—
That part we experience that tests our courage.
Without the need to overcome adversity,
Prosperity would not be so sweet a package.

If we had no winter, spring would not be as pleasant.
(How would we know when it arrived?)
Adversity has the effect of eliciting talents
To overcome one's condition and thrive!

"A man is insensible to the relish of prosperity,"
So states Sa'di, a Persian poet of old.
He finishes the thought: "... till he has tasted adversity."
(This is 13th century wisdom to behold.)

FEASTING ON ANGER

Anger is fun.
Of the seven deadly sins,
anger is perhaps
the most delicious.

Licking wounds over
grievances long past;
Getting your tongue around
thoughts of future face-offs;

Savoring the thought of pain...
that which you received,
and the getting even...
the gotten and the given.

The chief drawback is:
What you are wolfing down
is none other than yourself.
The skeleton at the feast is you.

MAKING CHANGES IN YOUR LIFE

Take a look around you; what do you see?
Then look inside for a reading as well.
Everything you find is there for a reason.
The reason: we create our own heaven and hell.

Everything you have in your life you've created
With your thoughts and feelings and actions to date.
If you desire change your life can be different
By changing those things—it's not too late.

In life you'll find we have reasons or results.
We tend to rationalize away our blues.
But please take a look at 'rational lies' and know
That believing them does not make them true.

As Norman Cousins said so well, and was quoted:
One's 'death is not the greatest loss in life.
The greatest loss,' he says with much authority,
'Is what dies inside us while we live.' (in strife).

If you want some things in your life to be changed,
To be different and better for your peace of mind,
You'll have to work from the inside, and change
Your thoughts and actions which to you have been unkind.

THE IMPORTANCE OF BEING HERE NOW

Carpe diem! Seize the day!
Pay attention to what you are doing!
Don't let the precious days slip away
And be lost in the pursuing.

Each day you must try to place your focus
On each moment, pay attention now!
Glean what you can from every second.
Stay aware! Stay awake! You know how!

Don't let your days slip by ten by ten,
And wonder to yourself where they went.
Stay alert, stay alive, and focus on the moment.
Your life will be filled with enjoyment.

POETRY

It's the revelation
Of a sensation
That the poet
(Wouldn't you know it)
Believes to be
Felt only interiorly
And personal to
The writer who
... **writes it.**

It's the interpretation
Of a sensation
That was fueled by
A poet's sigh
And believed to be
Shared mutually
And personal to
The lucky one who
... **reads it.**